# THE
# Log Home
# Book

# THE Log Home Book

Written and photographed by

Ralph Kylloe

GIBBS SMITH

TO ENRICH AND INSPIRE HUMANKIND

First Edition
14 13 12 11 10    5 4 3 2 1

Text © 2010 Ralph Kylloe
Photographs © 2010 Ralph Kylloe

Published by
Gibbs Smith
P.O. Box 667
Layton, Utah 84041

1.800.835.4993 orders
www.gibbs-smith.com

Design by Renee Bond
Printed and bound in China
Gibbs Smith books are printed on either recycled, 100% post-
consumer waste, FSC-certified papers or on paper produced from
a 100% certified sustainable forest/controlled wood source.

Library of Congress Control Number:  2010928548

ISBN 13: 978-1-4236-1708-2
ISBN 10: 1-4236- 1708-8

*Previous overleaf: The front porch of a trapper's cabin is home to a mint-condition glider from Old Hickory.*

*Facing: An ultra-long coffee table can accommodate a game of Chinese checkers at one end while someone else looks at a photo scrapbook on the other. No need to worry about scratches: the table was custom made from recycled pine.*

# Contents

# Introduction

When I was in the third and fourth grades, I lived with my family in the small town of Pardeville, Wisconsin. At that time, we struggled, like many families, to make ends meet. But as an adult my memories of that period in my life are softened by the thoughts of my daily summertime fishing activities. There were two lakes in town, and every day that the sun shined I made my way down to the lower lake with my friend Richard Deitman. As eight-year-olds, we would dig in the earth for worms and collect enough to last for another evening of fishing.

At around four in the afternoon, Richard and I made our way to the end of an old wooden pier that creaked and groaned as we settled in for a late afternoon of fishing. Neither of us had good gear. We would buy four hooks for a nickel and took care not to lose them. Our fishing poles were probably secondhand, and the reels often became stuck because we didn't have the proper lubrication to keep them finely tuned. For bobbers, we both used small twigs tied to our lines.

The fishing was extraordinary! Each evening we would catch fifty or so blue gills, sunfish or perch. We kept several of them each night, and I was proud to return home after sundown with dinner for the evening.

Years later and back in Chicago, I joined the local Boys Club, where I traveled with many other inner-city kids to different summer camps. It was there where I enjoyed campfires and camp songs and marshmallows, ghost stories, canoe trips and hot dogs. In time I became a counselor at different camps around the country and continued my love affair with cabins and camps and the entire vacation experience.

Memories of these experiences bring meaning to my life now, and dealing in rustic furnishings for cabins and camps has become my livelihood. It's memories such as these that each of us associate with the cabins, lodges, resorts and ranches that we all love. These are the places that allow us to discover who we are. These are places of peace and comfort.

I've been photographing rustic homes for many years and have authored more than twenty books on the subject of rustic homes, furniture, and living. This book shares some of my favorite photographs, images that conjure my own memories of time spent at the cabin.

I hope the settings in this book recall some of your own cabin experiences. There are decorating and design ideas galore here. Take some inspiration for your own cabin, even if it's nestled in the middle of a big city or blossoming behind the auspices of a suburban home. After all, cabin is a real place, but it can be anywhere—even in a corner of your mind.

*Prized collections of accessories and art often take up residence in cabins. Pitchers, pack baskets, tins and the like give each cabin home personality.*

Everyone knows the importance of a good first impression. What people see as you greet them at your cabin door and bring them inside gives them an immediate feeling of your cabin's personality. Moreover, a staircase winding from the entranceway to the second-floor bedrooms adds to the feeling of welcome.

As for the door itself, nothing beats the strength and

# Entryways & Staircases

*There is plenty to attract interest in this stairway nook: colorful buckets of flowers, a collection of branding irons hanging from a bronze chandelier, and a flag draped over one post for a pop of color. One small drawback of cabins is that the expanses of wood are often dark, necessitating attention to lighting and added color.*

security of antique oak. If you happen to find a door with a beveled or stained-glass window, you'll be lucky indeed. However, the most dramatic front doors are those custom made, with carvings of wildlife, fish or pine boughs. A great way to blend your home with its natural surrounds is to have a door crafted from logs cut on your own property. For existing cabins, you can even order a custom door frame (two vertical sides plus a head piece) and attach it to the outside of your existing frame to avoid a major construction job.

Staircases are as unique as the materials they're made from. Log banisters are traditionally expected in cabins, and they have personality galore. You can switch it up with wrought-iron or wood balusters carved with nature motifs. In additional to being functional, staircases can be works of art.

9

A handcrafted twig mosaic door is punctuated with pinecones.

Facing: A side table supporting matching lamps and an interesting box chest is flanked by two Indiana hickory chairs. Light from the open door illuminates the painting.

*Facing: Manka's Inverness Lodge in Marin County, California, has individual cabins for rent. The chairs at the front door make it easy for guests to visit and greet passersby. A luxe evergreen wreath dresses up an otherwise plain but classic wood door.*

*Left: This potbellied stove appears to be functional, but even if it weren't hooked up to gas, what a delightful personality it gives to the nook by the stairway. Navajo rugs and camp blankets always have a home in cabin decor.*

Left: A classic symmetrical entrance has double pole columns—out front and at the side of the door—as well as flanking side lights. Note the impact of accessories: imagine this porch without the antlers, hanging planter and flag. A dormer window reflects the surroundings.

Above: Balusters arranged in a geometric design dress up what could have been an ordinary staircase. Because there's a landing partway up, the entire staircase is visible from the main floor great room.

Scandinavian motifs and baluster style were employed in this home. Notice that the motifs in the climbing balusters are slightly different from those in the upper railing.

Facing: A staircase climbs to the second story in the center of the room. The stringers, stairs and structural center beam are all red pine. The newel posts and center support posts were cut from apple trees years before the staircase was made. Oak banisters came from trees cut on the property when the house was built. Caribou antlers form loose balusters.

Walking into these two settings from outside would be two very different experiences. In one, simple sheaths of twigs decorate the entry into a library. This setting exudes a feeling of rest and relaxation.

Facing: Opening the door onto a collection of fishing creels and pack baskets would send a completely different message. Conversation would quickly turn to fishing, and a night's activity might be fly-tying in preparation for an early start the next day.

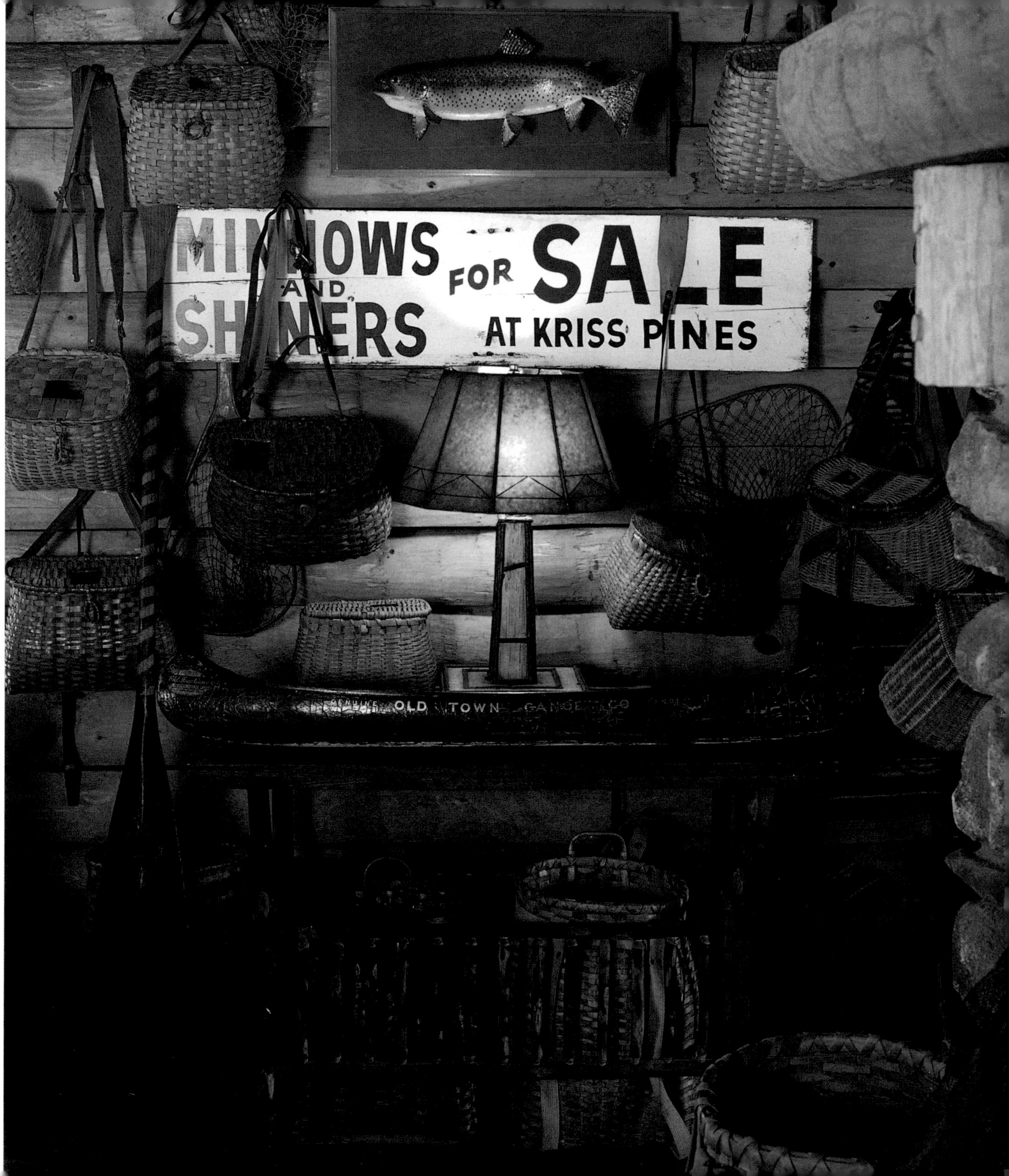
AND
FOR SALE
AT KRISS PINES
OLD TOWN

*Facing:* The front door of this cabin opens onto the expansive great room. A short wall acts as a divider for the entrance, while a fantastically grotesque chandelier of natural driftwood lights the way.

*Left:* Natural branches set between lodgepole posts give this staircase a contemporary look. Here again, the staircase is backdrop to a seating area. The chairs have an old Spanish colonial style; a bulbous table base is a good contrast with the slender chair arms; and animal hides make the setting a little bit exotic.

Natural materials make all the difference in these two staircases. Left, deer antlers become decorative balusters for an otherwise functional staircase. Above, a burled lodgepole stringer supports the half-round log staircase, while twisted juniper supports the stringer and also makes an artistic banister.

*Alike but different. In both homes, thick lodgepole pines support the staircase. Natural growth features and organic shapes in the wood are featured and set in ways that show off their beauty. Here is evidence of what the artistic eye of a skilled wood craftsmen can bring to the beauty of a home when allowed to make decisions about use of materials during the building process.*

Rustic living rooms and great rooms have the capacity to renew the spirit. They are designed to provide comfort and to foster a sense of community and family. Here you can let down your guard and relax. People only a few blinks away from sleep can find peace and solitude in a comfy chair or on an overstuffed sofa. Great rooms are ideal for casual, intimate conversations.

# Living & Great Rooms

*This sitting room is awash in hand-crafted luxury. A log chair and foot rest that mimic cabin construction make an ideal place for a nap by the fire. At left, the fireplace mantel is made from burled pine. Handmade furniture pieces boast meticulous twig applique.*

Comfort and livability are the keys to a great living area. Feet and beverages are not out of place on the coffee tables. We invite pets to cuddle up with us on any one of the chairs or couches. Lamp shades of mica, glass, cloth or parchment sport a host of rustic scenes. Canoes hang from the ceiling, and the fireplace makes us cozy on a chilly day.

Rustic-style couches that are comfortable—apart from those made of Indiana hickory or in mission style—are very difficult to find. Consequently, many homes today have new upholstered sofas that are often the focal point of the room. The most comfortable always seem to be those that are oversized and give one the sensation of sinking into a cloud or pillow. Many rustic homes have sleeper sofas for guests who happen to show up on weekends for an extended visit.

Four ample-sized leather arm-chairs face a central point in this living room to make a cordial conversation area. One might think this cabin owner relishes retreat time with family and friends.

*Facing:* Off to the side of the main living space of another home, a small table becomes a fun work area, enhanced by a collection of antiques: pack baskets, painted wooden ducks and miscellaneous other items. There's no doubt about the kinds of recreational sports this cabin owner enjoys.

Facing: A small one-room cabin, accessible only by horseback, makes good use of space. The eating area is also functional for talking over the day's ride, while two berth beds with storage drawers beneath offer a cozy night's sleep. Antique barn wood, a few antique collectibles and authentic Navajo rugs turn this cabin into a classy destination.

Left: At the opposite end of the size spectrum, a grand living room is fitted with overstuffed couches and thick-cushioned chairs arranged in several intimate seating groups.

*Left: A small living room is furnished with hickory chairs and settees. Damaged Navajo rugs were cut up and made into throw pillows. Taxidermy and vintage signs provide interest from every viewpoint.*

*Above: Classic western ambience is the order of the day in* this living room. The red leather furniture pieces are Thomas Molesworth originals; this style, which he created in the 1930s, was prevalent in dude ranches of the period. Native American artifacts and period paintings contribute to the old-timey atmosphere.

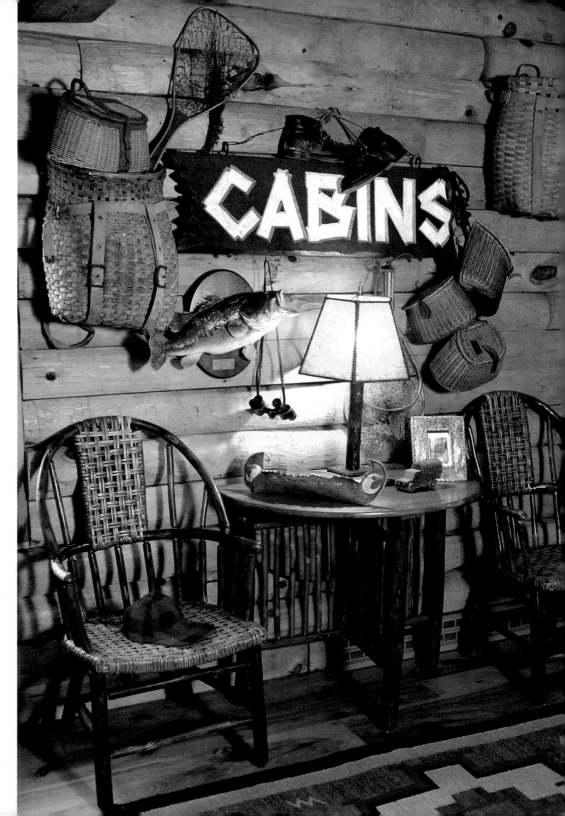

A vignette area in this living room is anchored by a rustic "Cabins" sign on the wall. The Old Hickory furniture consists of two captain's chairs and a drop-leaf gate-leg table. Fishing creels, a net and an Adirondack basket round out the appeal to fishermen.

Facing: More furniture in the style of Thomas Molesworth fills out a great room that holds several tables, ample chairs and couches, and still has enough open floor space for kids to play or to host a line dance! The room-size rug underneath the sofas is from the Ganado region of the Navajo Nation.

Facing: A combination sitting/ sleeping room at this cabin at Manka's Inverness Lodge has a fisherman theme. Tightly organized, it still has comfortable seating on an overstuffed couch or in 1930s Old Hickory chairs.

Left: A living room in New Hampshire also features Old Hickory furniture and related memorabilia, including an original furniture advertisement dating from 1924. Ever-present: the classic Navajo rug defines the area for the furniture grouping.

*Left: Scandinavian influence enters this living room by way of the tall cabinet on the left and the table used as a console behind the sofa. The fireplace, made from rock found on the property, anchors the living room.*

*Above: Leather-upholstered furniture, an inviting fireplace and a telescope for watching wildlife are the markings of a classic Rocky Mountain cabin living room.*

A tasteful selection of furniture and accessories gives this great room an elegant ambience. Breaking from the usual cabin colors, the owners' choice of green fabric for the sofas really takes it upscale for a look that is more contemporary than old. Even though the space is used for dining, cooking, casual living or entertaining, furnishings have been kept under control so the room doesn't feel at all crowded.

*Facing: Molesworth furniture takes center stage in this living room. All four pieces in the foreground are Molesworth. Applied half-round wood pieces were one of his hallmarks. Bear sculptures are a favorite of the homeowner. Contrasting the western look and adding some sophistication are two period chairs with white upholstery. The Indian blanket hanging on the wall is from the Germantown period. Both red weavings reinforce the red color scheme, which is a very traditional color used to brighten cabin interiors.*

*Facing: While seeming totally western, this living room furniture also speaks of the Victorian era. This is a style that is often portrayed in western movies and TV shows and was seen in hotels of the Old West.*

*Left: There's nothing like hand-made furniture to bring humor and personality to a cabin. Whether created by an artist or an amateur, one-of-a-kind pieces are sure to spark conversation and stimulate admiration.*

Fireplaces and fires are an integral part of the rustic atmosphere. No camp scene is complete without one. Fires are so important as a means of bonding and relaxing that in the past, if a house did not have a fireplace, artificial logs and red light bulbs were combined to fabricate a fire in an artificial fireplace complete with a mantel.

# Fireplaces

*The two most imposing elements of a fireplace are the rock surround and the mantel. Each is truly a work of art. The log burls that make up this mantel were scouted from the high mountains on horseback.*

Real fireplaces need andirons and firescreens. In the past, rustic andirons took the shape of owls, pine trees, Indian tepees and other creative designs. Many firescreens were also adorned with rustic scenes, including log homes and fishing and forest panoramas, which were applied to the wire mesh that protects the room from embers. Both rustic andirons and firescreens are being reproduced today, or originals can be found at flea markets, at auctions or in antiques shops.

Fireplace mantels are as important to rustic decor as fireplaces. Trophies, either won, caught or bought, look totally at home gracing the shelves above a fireplace. Photos of all sorts, personal memorabilia, snowshoes, skis, canoe paddles and other artifacts fit in perfectly with the rustic feel of a fireplace.

The fireplace is king in almost every cabin living room. Even if the cabin is summer-use only, a crackling fire draws the crowd and mesmerizes even the wiggliest of children.

The fireplace above left was built by the dry-stack method, while the one above right uses mortar as part of the design. Each fireplace is the work of a talented stonemason.

This off-centered contemporary fireplace is located in the King Pacific Lodge, a floating resort south of the Queen Charlotte Islands.

*Artistry is evident in this twig fireplace mantel. The unique firescreen design further supports a clean, contemporary look for this home.*

*Facing: A heavily burled mantel-piece reinforces the western theme in this room.*

*Facing: How classically simple! Yellow birch logs support the mantel and frame the rock fireplace in a room at the Lake Placid Lodge.*

*Left: One end of a small stone cabin is centered by a slightly protruding fireplace. This room exudes the qualities of innovative handcraftsmanship.*

This fireplace is found in the main lodge of the The Big Hole River Ranch in southern Montana. Due to the rectangular shape of the stones, the fireplace remains flat against the wall and doesn't protrude into the room, as many fireplaces do. The mantel is a narrow wood slab.

Facing: An upside-down keystone rests on two vertical columns of rocks and boulder. This surround is a fine specimen of innovation, combining rocks of various sizes in a pleasing design.

Facing: Reclaimed wood used in unique combinations with stone makes this newly built fishing cabin look as old as the hills— and that's what the architect intended. Arranging the rocks in just-so order makes everything come out even on top.

Left: A half-height corner fireplace is big enough to take the chill off cold nights. The stone hearth is large enough for seating.

Prairie moss rock quarried in *Harlowton, Montana,* is the *stone used to create the fireplace in this exclusive fishing camp. The design is simple yet exquisite.*

*Facing: An all-stone fireplace utilizes a keystone arch at the top of the opening. The pressure of the smaller stones on the sides against the larger stone at the top of the key holds the entire arched group in place.*

*Facing: This fireplace has a broader base than top; the rocks step in as the structure rises from the floor. The mouth being somewhat large makes tending the fire a bit easier.*

*Left: Stone type and color, along with the fireplace design, give this fireplace a contemporary modern look that complements the modern design of the building.*

The mason gave this new fireplace a sleek, tapered design.
Tremendous skill goes into select-
ing the right sizes and shapes of
stone to achieve the desired look.

*Facing:* The tapered form, over-
hangs on the mantel, arched
keystone and cascading footings
make this a classic fireplace.

Facing, top: A dry-stacked fireplace in a small cabin at first seems to overtake the room when juxtaposed to the built-in beds on either side. But the fireplace actually serves as a divider between two sleeping places, allowing each person a feeling of privacy even though they're sharing the same space.

Facing, bottom: A small fireplace in a suite at the old Lake Placid lodge saw plenty of use over the years before this cabin was destroyed by fire.

Left: Logs for the fire wait in a recessed nook. In addition to being used for storage, such a recessed space could be engineered for cooking.

Rustic kitchens and dining rooms need to be versatile: here tasty meals are served, the paper is read, board games are played, and the fishing tackle for tomorrow's outing can be cleaned and prepared.

Rustic tables can be small and dainty—perfect for breakfast by the window or a candlelight dinner for two. Or they can be massive—large enough to serve a

# Kitchens & Dining Rooms

banquet to the neighborhood. The larger tables often have legs made from huge apple-tree branches, rhodo-dendron roots, or cedar or birch trees. Small tables are often scaled-down versions of their heftier cousins and are occasionally adorned with twig supports to add grace and sturdiness, as well as an aesthetic touch.

Antique tables can fit comfortably in a rustic setting. You need not feel compelled to refinish your table because it has stains or scratches or someone's initials carved in it. Old and rugged is charming and adds to the lived-in effect. If you'd rather have a new table, a range of sizes and shapes are available from rustic builders around the country. Old or new, don't forget to wax, oil or varnish your table once a year to keep it waterproof.

*A stunning handcrafted cupboard curves to fit snugly against the wall of a circular dining room. Wicker and hickory chairs take their places around the dining table.*

When planning meals at the cabin, the cook is often preparing for a gang. So it's no surprise that people want the conveniences of stainless steel ranges, easy-to-clean counter space and access to all the action while preparing the food. For tables, though, whether they seat two, four or a dozen, wood reigns supreme. Here are juxtaposed examples of casual and formal cabin dining areas.

*Facing: An old wooden table has been painted with a checkerboard design. When not in service for lunch, this corner doubles as a game area or fly-tying station.*

*Left: Here is another case of a multiple-use table. Pull up a chair and enjoy a cup of joe and a sandwich, or hang out with buddies and swap fishing tales.*

*Left: Vintage-look appliances might not be right for every cabin, but in the right kitchen, this look can really enhance your cabin experience. Who knows—they might even make the food more wholesome and better tasting. This kitchen sings with a mix of periods and styles.*

*Above: "A table by the window, please." If the space is small, the view from the table is as big as the outdoors.*

In an Adirondack dining room, hickory furniture is the mainstay. Six vintage Old Hickory dining chairs surround the table, while vintage camp signs and other memorabilia decorate the walls. As in most cabins, the dining area is multipurpose.

Facing: Flexible seating is provided in this all-purpose area. The round table can be moved into the corner, where built-in benches become banquette seating.

*Left:* Counter seating is the order of the day in this kitchen, where four bar stools snug up to the bar. This creates an optimal situation for the cook to be involved in all the pre-meal conversation or to pass a bowl of potatoes to someone for peeling. An ever-growing collection of antique camp signs and other related cabin accessories tell any guest that this is a fun place to hang out.

*Above:* The kitchen island was covered with bark-on hemlock. The counter tops are made from three-inch white pine slabs.

Facing: All in one: cooking, eating and sleeping are done in one small room. The table and chairs are by Charles Limbert, from the Arts and Crafts period.

Left: Belly up to the bar, boys. The seat on the bar stool is pretty tiny, so you wouldn't want to stay here long; but for coming and going, grabbing a cold one on a hot day, this is an ideal serving station. And a sidepiece like this, with an icy cooler or a refrigerator nearby, could take the pressure off the kitchen area where someone might be making preparations for the next meal.

*Left:* This colorful dining room rests in a beautiful 1930s Adirondack lakeside home. Antique and contemporary rustic furniture and accessories give diners plenty to look at. In addition to the six chairs at the table, a few more seats are available at the shelf bar on the right.

*Above:* In a luxury setting, the dining table seats ten people comfortably. It's a good idea to have a few extra chairs nearby for occasions when the number of guests outstrips the usual capacity. In lieu of squeezing more chairs around the table, a second table can be set up for service—just like at Thanksgiving.

Handcrafted cabinetry, stainless steel appliances and a sleek granite countertop give this kitchen an upscale modern look. The flooring is soapstone tiles and the bar chairs are hickory.

Facing: This great room has ample space for a dining table as well as other seating. Meals can be served at the counter or the table. Pillows in the lower foreground hint at some overstuffed furniture in the dining area. A vintage European cabinet stands guard in an adjoining passageway and holds a collection of Indian dolls.

Facing, above left and right: Two cabins provide for romantic fireside suppers.

Facing, below: A cooking nook in the corner of a great room is enclosed on three sides. This is a perfect arrangement for a cook who doesn't want anybody else salting his stew or tasting his fish before it's ready to serve. Still, no one is shut out of the conversation or activities taking place all around the house.

Left: What appears to be an heirloom mahogany dining set also serves as a display area for a collection of bronzes and other artwork. A lodgepole pine door frame gives the small kitchenette a degree of separation.

Bedrooms in the rustic style are havens from the outside world. They are places of longing and fantasy that bring us closer to nature. Handcrafted, one-of-a-kind beds made from logs, gnarly branches and twigs give us the feeling of being cradled in a tree or nest.

Rustic furniture has an attitude of ruggedness, independence and individuality. The most extreme and wild

# Bedrooms

rustic beds are made out of huge limbs and adorned with all the wild branches, twigs and buds that they maintained in the wild. Styles of bedroom furniture range from the absolutely simple Shaker style to the twisting, organic forms of log furniture. Four-poster beds are constructed of hickory, birch, cedar or other woods that are accessible to the builder. Bunks are particularly functional for cabins because they maximize the bedroom space to allow for big family vacations.

Bedrooms are the most personal rooms in our homes. They give away secrets about the people who reside there. They are rooms for quiet times and intimacy. They hold our most personal belongings, and we go to them to be rejuvenated and refreshed. Whether for just one person or a gang of kids, bedrooms in the rustic style are cozy, warm and inviting.

*Free-form bunk beds are made from scraps of lodgepole and jack pine. Gnarly!*

Lightweight fabric draped over the four hardwood posts and a string of delicate lights turn rugged into romantic.

Facing: The author's daughter adores her Adirondack bedroom, which includes antique hickory furniture and whimsical bird accessories.

Facing: Cabin red is the theme here. The bed cover and curtains appear to be of similar, if not the same, red-and-black wool fabric, available at many outdoor stores. The curtain rods are two-inch-thick yellow birch poles. Deer antlers hold the rod aloft. The pack basket resting on the floor might be used for laundry.

Left: An antique four-poster bed is covered with a 1930s American crazy quilt.

*Left:* Red-and-black check carries the color scheme here again, this time with a ruffled flounce. But this room is clearly for fun and play as much as it is for sleeping. The foursome resting on the bed have probably heard more secrets than most. The whimsical bed frame is birch. An ornate root mirror frame makes a big statement on the wall.

*Above:* Pastel walls with a faux finish are a nice accent to the ancient timbers. A custom armoire and a bark-on bed further the rustic ambiance, while upholstered chairs and a room-size rug give the bedroom all the comforts of home.

Handcrafted artistry is evident in the bed and matching rail of applied pole high on the wall. Imagine yourself in here with just the glow of the fire and low light from the stunning wreath chandelier.

Facing: Birch bark and logs give this Lake Placid Lodge cabin an Adirondack ambience. The bed is yellow birch, while the ceiling is lined with sheets of white birch bark and the walls are lined with white birch and cedar logs.

*Facing: A bureau from the Hickory Furniture Company and Hudson Bay blankets on the wall beside it all date from the 1930s.*

*Left: In master bedrooms, the fireplace is king.*

*Above: A couple of daybeds turn this bunk room into a game room, chat room or reading room.*

*Left: A subtle Native American theme enters this bedroom by way of the textiles on the bench and floor, as well as the hand-painted decorative pillow and a few well-placed artifacts.*

*Above: A contemporary bunkhouse is furnished with lodgepole pine bunks adorned with colorful bedding. The bent-willow armchair is a classic gypsy design.*

*Facing:* Nostalgic western motifs give this room a masculine feel: Buffalo Bill and Indian chief painted carvings on the headboard and footboard, hide (or faux-hide) on the bed and chair, a cowboy cutout on the chair back, horse-and-rider motifs on the lamp shade and a contemporary western painting on the wall.

*Above:* Another example of the western theme, executed more simply in the blankets, rug and chair weavings as well as the wild animal motifs on the chair side and lamp shade.

Facing: Although this bedroom is obviously large (i.e., king-size bed and room enough for a sofa), the tendency to fill it up is tempered by a built-in bookcase, matching nightstands and a fold-out bench attached to the footboard.

Left: If you're dreaming of a night in the forest, this room is the place to stay! The burled lodgepole bed is sturdy enough to last for generations. Two moose mounts keep watch for intruders.

*Left:* Simply elegant—fallow deer and mule deer antlers adorn the upholstered leather headboard and footboard.

*Above:* Not all cabins need to have rustic furniture. An heirloom mahogany bed with exquisitely turned and embellished posts is a standout in this master bedroom, while several rugs cover the floor and a few odd furniture pieces fill out the accommodations.

Playful and funky are good words to describe cabin bathrooms. Vanities are made from tree stumps or barn wood, and the cabinet doors might be made of barn wood or decorated with twig mosaics. Mirrors framed in antlers, twigs or birch bark find their way into the bathroom, as do a few art objects, like wildlife sculptures and paintings. Towel racks and paper holders are often unique as

# Bathrooms

well, being made from branches, wrought iron or rusty old finds.

The luxury of a long soak in a claw-foot tub after a day of vigorous hiking, fishing or snowshoeing seems perfectly suited to cabin life. On the other hand, a quick shower or scrub-up in the sink gets the cabin guest quickly on his or her way to the next activity. Double, and even triple, sinks are especially handy for serving the needs of bunk room buddies.

Whether used as a temporary retreat from the clamor of the day, or just for the occasional personal need, a visit to a cabin bathroom always gives one the feeling of days gone by. And in our hurry-up world of lightning-speed everything, a little bit of the old times does a body good.

*Barn wood and burled logs form an attractive vanity, while applied poles take a slab door from ordinary to extraordinary.*

Sheets of birch bark are used as wallpaper here, and decoration is applied directly to the wall with twigs and mirrors. Note the canoe toothbrush holder.

*Facing: This bath space is simply luxurious. A claw-foot tub offers a long, hot soak and an antique rocker made of willow shoots and oak invites a second party in for a private conversation.*

Facing: This bathroom boasts an unusual wainscot of stacked flat rock.

Left: At one end of the bath, a handsome door provides entrance to a glorious shower and steam room.

*Facing:* A rock-sheathed tub provides the bather with magical transport to natural pools and waterfalls. At sunset, golden light pours through the window.

*Left:* A diamond-pattern twig mosaic dresses up the doors of a vanity made from vintage barn wood. A wall-size mirror reveals wood slats on the ceiling and makes the room seem larger.

*Above:* Necessity is the mother of invention, they say. Even though necessity doesn't dictate here, this washtub basin is pretty clever.

Burled logs hold the cabinet in place. Colorful applied twig mosaics make the cabinet doors stellar.

Facing: A unique root-base washstand is made of lodgepole pine.

*Facing: Drawer pulls and han-
dles in this bathroom are crafted
of leather and silver in western
motifs. A chestnut countertop
holds a copper basin. Rows of
applied log decorate the mirror
and cabinet front.*

*Left: A burled vanity with slab
countertop gives this small bathroom rustic ambience, while the
burled mirror doubles the impact
of a colorful work of art.*

*Facing: A fisherman might be tempted to stay a while in this bathroom, with its unique fishing-rod mirror, hand-carved fish sculpture and shadow box of bobbers.*

*Left: Scarred antique barn wood is the prevalent construction material in this bathroom.*

*Above: Sponged rust-red walls make this bathroom sing.*

Traditionally, cabin porches are places to repair an outboard motor, work on fishing gear, enjoy a favorite beverage and commiserate with others over the "one that got away." More elaborate rustic porches are homes to fascinating plants, hot tubs and barbecue grills.

Rest and relaxation, however, are the uses that all good porches have in common. Some are large

# Outbuildings, Porches & Patios

enough for picnic tables, which means they often host brunches and aperitifs, as well as championship checkers matches, poker games and various forms of artistic endeavor. Porches may also harbor several hanging planters, bird feeders, dog bowls and beds for pets in need of a snooze.

Many patios and porches have floors made from cedar logs, fieldstone, driftwood or other natural materials. Woods used in constructing railings and banisters often retain their original twists, contortions and connecting appendages.

When coming from the outdoors and preparing to enter the house, the porch is a good buffer, maintaining a significant feeling of continuity with the outdoors.

And, of course, the scene from the patio is everything!

*Antique Old Hickory chairs with extra spindles reflect influence of the Arts and Crafts movement (around 1875–1920). Adirondack baskets and a few other collectibles fill the space with nostalgia and color.*

*Left: A covered patio is simply set with hickory chairs, a table and a settee. Woven seats of any type—cane, rattan or wicker—should be protected from the weather for longer life.*

*Above: A mint-condition Old Hickory glider with rattan canning on the seat is complemented by a small side table with weaving that serves to both decorate and strengthen the piece.*

*An early porch glider hangs from its frame on chains and probably dates from the early 1920s. Signs and other accessories make this porch corner a charming place to while away some time.*

*Facing: Chairs of different shapes and waves fill this classic Adirondack back porch. Rain or shine, there is space for some of the furniture; the rest is pulled inside during inclement weather.*

*Left:* A forest green–painted floor provides a solid ground for geometric balusters, armchairs, an umbrella stand and a birch swing in the far back.

*Above:* Even the tiniest cabin (this one houses bunks for kids) wants a little patio out front. This one is hung with an assortment of old tools and memorabilia.

*Facing: Both old and new pieces of history furniture grace this front porch. From this setting, people can coax the sun up (or put it to bed) in grand style.*

*Left: A tree runs through it. On a porch at Manka's Inverness Lodge is a pair of Old Hickory steamer chairs made in the 1930s, each with a leg rest that can double as a side table.*

*Left:* A platform patio lets the rain run off, so guests can enjoy a dry evening sit even if the day has been rainy. Openings in the rail on three sides make coming and going ultra convenient. The cabin itself is covered in bark-on hemlock.

*Above:* Four pieces of this porch furniture (settee, ottoman and two chairs) are collectible "prison" furniture, made by the inmates of the state prison in Putnamville, Indiana, beginning in the 1930s.

This artist's cabin in the West is bermed into the hillside and has no room for a formal patio. However, from a lounge chair placed lengthwise on the flagstone walkway, the view is grand and inspiring.

Facing: These classically rustic covered porches illustrate two takes on porch railings. One features geometric lines and angles, the other organic lines and shapes.

*Left: Contemporary teak patio furniture is perfectly at home in the mountains. An expansive stone patio provides space for the sunbathers and shade lovers alike.*

*Above: Outside the east entrance to Yellowstone National Park, the Crossed Sabres Ranch has ample porch seating for plenty of guests.*

*Facing: The romantic and restorative benefits of private balconies are not to be ignored.*

*Left: Munchkins would love this backyard shed made of bark-on cedar.*

*Left: Hickory furniture under a wide porch overhang is the order of the day.*

*Above: A west-facing porch is the perfect spot for sipping evening drinks and watching the sunset.*

With wall hangings, flowers, a table and seating options, this porch feels like an outdoor room.

Facing, top: The living space of a trapper's cabin is expanded by the porch.

Facing, bottom: If privacy is what is wanted, this porch will provide it. It is tucked under the overhanging eaves and secluded by plantings.

*Facing, top, and left: Two views of a fishing cabin show the real benefits of the covered porch/ patio: it faces the pond and turns into an outdoor storytelling room at the end of every day.*

*Facing, bottom: Okay, probably nobody wants to park a chair on this porch, but the fact that it's there helps keep your trousers from dragging in the mud on the way to the outhouse.*

*Previous spread: The ultimate porch: enough room for games by day and dancing under the stars at night.*

*Moose and elk antlers make this one-off chair sturdy and surprisingly comfortable.*